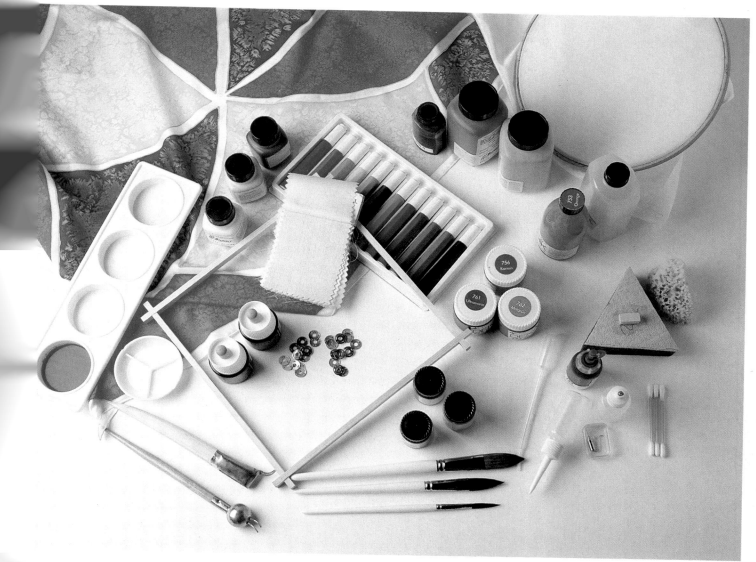

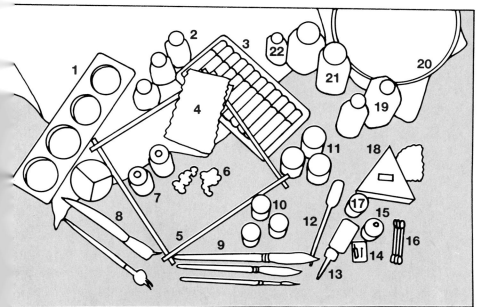

Key to photograph

1 palettes; **2** Dupont fabric paints; **3** textile markers; **4** silk swatches; **5** square frame; **6** 3-pronged pins; **7** Pebeo silk paints; **8** batik tjantings; **9** silk painting brushes; **10** Deka fabric paints; **11** Deka silk paints; **12** plastic dropper; **13** plastic bottle with dropper; **14** gutta pen; **15** gutta bottle and pen; **16** cotton wool buds; **17** Deka fabric paint; **18** sponges; **19** Dupont serti and Deka silk paint; **20** tambour frame; **21** Dupont fabric paints; **22** Deka fabric paint

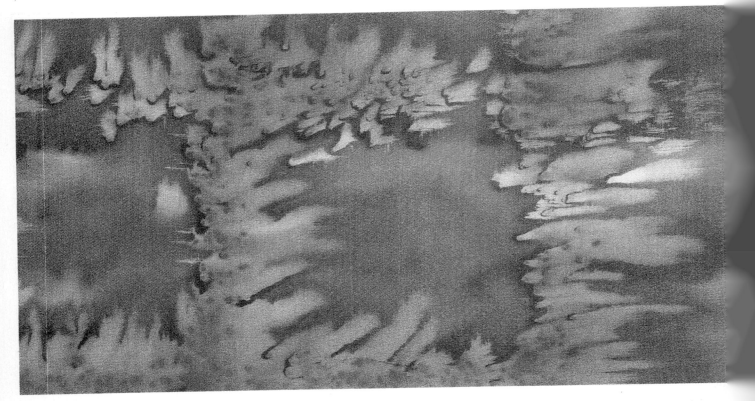

Above: Free flow paint with salt added for a 'tartan' effect on Antung silk

Salt fixing

Salt is a natural dye fixative and when used with other chemicals it makes an effective fixative bath for painted cloth. Use salt as an extra precaution against fading in painted fabrics for upholstery and curtains which are exposed to direct sunlight. Paint the cloth with a 50% salt, 50% water solution after painting, let dry then wash out.

Applicators

All the techniques in this book require special tools for applying the paints. Using the wrong tools may lead to unsatisfactory results, so always make sure you have the equipment listed in each section.

Brushes

Paint brushes are used for fabric painting and for applying barrier or fixing solutions. Avoid sable or natural bristles because textile paints and rough fabrics tend to wear them out quickly. Instead, choose synthetic fibre brushes, which are cheaper and harder wearing. You'll need a variety of sizes. Japanese ink brushes are particularly useful, while household paint brushes are suitable for heavy duty fabric.

Special silk painting brushes are available from craft shops.

Pipettes

Some techniques require paint to be dripped on to the fabric. A pipette is used for this. If you cannot obtain one, use a drinking straw or a chemist's eye-dropper. Keep a different pipette for each colour, and always wash both tube and squeezer in warm, soapy water after use.

Sponges

Sponges are used for fabric printing. Natural sponges are best, although they are expensive. Nylon sponges cost less but tend to be short-lived. Choose sponges with lots of surface holes, as it is the holes which leave the interesting imprint. Sponges can be cut with scissors into small pieces. Keep one sponge piece for each colour and clean them after use in clear, running water. Never use soap.

Plant sprays

These are ideal for covering large background areas. Set the nozzle at a fine spray and the faster you work, the more even the painting. Sprays are available from garden accessory shops. Choose sprays with adjustable nozzles which can be used to create a fine mist

or large, deliberate drops.

Tjanting

This tool of Indonesian origin is the traditional batik tool. It is used for drawing on fabric, using hot wax in the batik method. Brushes can also be used, but they quickly wear out.

Tjap

This rare Indonesian tool is used for printing hot wax designs on to fabric in the batik method.

Gutta pipette and pen

The gutta technique requires a gutta or serti pipette attached to a metal pen. This is secured with masking tape to the bottle and the gutta or serti solution is then squeezed onto the fabric, either as a barrier or as a decoration.

Cotton buds

These small sticks tipped with cotton-wool balls can be used to apply runny paint to fine silk.

Tooth and nail brushes

These create a rough brushed effect for backgrounds or specific designs. Long strokes applied in several layers give a three dimensional effect. Clean the brushes after use under running water.

Designer Tips 1

Working with paints

Paints are highly sensitive to direct heat and light. Always close the jars after use and store them in a cool place away from direct light and where they are out of children's reach.

Fabric paints will stain cloth permanently even before they are fixed, so protect your clothing and surrounding furnishings, carpets and curtains etc. with old newspapers. As accidents happen very easily, it is a good idea to keep paints on a tray in case of spillage.

Drying times
Different brands vary in their drying times. Always make sure the paint has dried completely before removing cloth from a frame or work surface. The drying process can be speeded up with a hand-held hair dryer, but do not expose the fabric to direct sunlight as this will fade and spoil the colours. Gutta and serti painted designs must also be perfectly dry before being ironed or fixed.

Coloured backgrounds
Colours look quite different against a painted background than against a white one, so test the contrast on a small piece of cloth first. (Use only printing dyes for dark backgrounds.)

Colour mixing
Keep a record of the proportions used when mixing colours. Use an eye-dropper and count the number of drops used of each colour. Always work from light to dark.

Look after brushes
Most fabric paints are water soluble, so clean brushes with warm water and a mild detergent. Careful rinsing is vital as any residue left in the brush clogs the fibres and will leave marks on your fabric. Oil paint is washed out with turpentine or white spirit.

A place to work
Choose a well-lit area to work in, away from direct sunlight, and cover your work table with a plastic cloth or old newspaper. (The ink on fresh newspaper leaves black smudges.) Some fabric painting techniques require a padded surface.

Paint spraying is best done outside, or in the bathroom, where surfaces can be cleaned down easily.

Useful equipment
Jars with lids and screw-tops are ideal for storing paints. The shelf life of paints is quite long provided they are not diluted with tap water and are kept in a cool place. Paints mixed together neat can be stored for re-use this way. Large glass jars and plastic food pots are handy for cleaning brushes.

Collect and store all sorts of fabrics, if not for painting, then for rags or pressing cloths. Scraps are ideal for experimenting with the different techniques before embarking on a major project.

Left: 'Labyrinth'. Gutta resist technique in primary colours on 50%/50% silk/cotton

Fabrics

In fabric painting, fabrics are to you like an artist's canvas and there are many to choose from, in different textures and compositions. In this chapter you will discover the qualities of different fabrics so that when you are ready to begin painting, you will choose the most suitable

It is important to choose the right fabric according to its weight, absorbency and texture. Man-made fibre fabrics have the advantage of being cheaper and easier to care for, but colours will not come out as bright or deep as they will on natural fabrics. Silk, cotton and wool are best for fabric painting. Silk in particular is renowned for its lustre, strength and absorbency of paint. There are several weights, textures and weaves to choose from.

Habotai
This is a smooth-textured silk suitable for scarves, fashionwear and for cushions. It comes in three weights 5mm (¹/₅in), 6mm (⁵/₁₆in) and 8mm (¹/₃in). The weight determines its density and thus its colour absorbency. The lightest weight, 5mm (¹/₅in) absorbs the most colour.

Silk Antung
This beautiful, medium-weight and fine textured, ivory-coloured fabric is used for fashion garments and home furnishings.

Silk twill
This medium-weight silk has a ridged texture and is suitable for both fashion garments and home furnishings.

Crêpe de chine
This beautiful silk is expensive and should be used for very special projects.

Zanza silk and silk von Shan
These are similar to Habotai, but silk von Shan has a semi-satin texture on the right side and a rough texture on the reverse.

Silk doupion
This fabric has a high shine and uneven texture which makes it ideal for hand-painting. It is suitable for clothing and home furnishings. Doupion comes in several weights.
    Other types of silk are available but

always check that the weight and texture matches that recommended by the paint manufacturer.

Cotton
Crisp, versatile, pure cotton fabrics must be washed first to remove unwanted manufacturer's finishes which will affect its absorbency. Washing will also take up any shrinkage. If 100% cotton fabrics cannot be obtained, choose polycotton with the minimum percentage of man-made fibre.
    Here are some cotton fabrics suitable for fabric painting.

Silk cotton This 50% silk, 50% cotton fabric is ideal for lightweight clothing and is machine-washable.

Cotton lawn This fabric is of high quality, but tends to be expensive. It is suitable for bed linen and for children's clothing.

Voilissima This type of cotton lawn is the traditional fabric used for batik.

Primissima is a fine quality cotton lawn.

Calico is a heavy-weight, unbleached, pure cotton fabric.

Bleached cotton is similar to calico, but is a bright white. It is ideal as an upholstery fabric.

Cotton voile This fabric is open-weave, sheer and light-weight, making it suitable for lining, backing and for shadow quilting.

Cotton mule This cotton is similar to voile, but is more open-weave and not as smooth.

Cotton drill is a heavy, dense cotton, similar to bleached cotton, but with a ridged texture. It is soft and strong.

Right: Gold gutta lines were applied first, then blue, yellow and red were sponged over. The design is on Habotai silk.

Other fabrics
Linen Both shirt linen and rougher open-weave linen are suitable for painting, but they are expensive and may be hard to find.

Wool fabrics are very absorbent so when using them always double the quantity of paint recommended.

Nun's veiling This 100% lambswool fabric is soft, light to medium-weight and is suitable for items such as scarves and for clothing. Nun's veiling can be machine washed at 40°C.

Mohair, tweed and cashmere These fabrics can be painted, but special paints designed to cope with this type of wool will be needed.

Synthetic fibre fabrics Synthetic fabrics come in different types, weights and textures, often similar in look and handle to natural fabrics. Always check the fibre content label before buying. The effect of painting will vary considerably between natural and synthetic fibres.

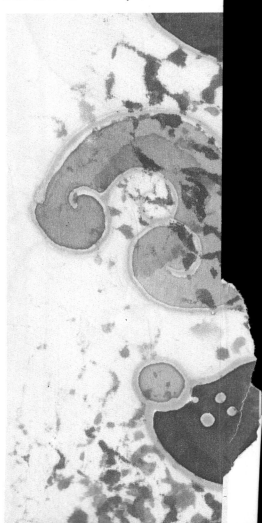

Designer Tips 2

Handling fabrics

The flame test is the best method of checking whether a fabric is natural or man-made. Hold a tiny scrap of material over a lighted candle. If it does not immediately flare up and the ash left behind is powdery, then the fabric is made of natural fibres.

If, however, the sample flames easily and the ash contains a plastic residue, this indicates the presence of man-made fibres.

Preparing fabric for painting

Always wash and iron pure cotton fabrics before painting or cutting to take up any shrinkage. Pre-wash fabrics which look glazed as artificial finishes prevent cloth from absorbing paint properly.

Cutting silk

Buy and mark a pair of very sharp scissors to be kept exclusively for silk. Blunt scissors will snag this delicate fabric.

Sewing with silk

Use silk or fine cotton thread for sewing silk. The thread should be of a similar weight to the fabric. Always use new sharp pins and new needles. For machine sewing, put a layer of acid-free tissue paper underneath fine silk cloth to avoid puckering under the foot. Take care to set the stitch according to the weight and texture of the fabric, and always finish silk garments and furnishings by hand. This gives the fabric a chance to hang naturally.

Washing and aftercare

Silk needs careful handling, so use medium hot water and very mild detergent such as wool soap, or have the fabric dry-cleaned. Take special care to rinse off all soap particles, as any left behind will leave permanent marks when the fabric is ironed.

Always leave silk to drip dry. Never wring it out as this will damage the filaments. Do not use a tumble drier.

Store silk in a dry place, covered with polythene or acid-free tissue paper.

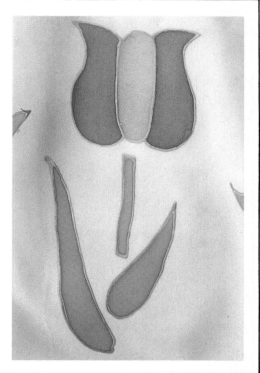

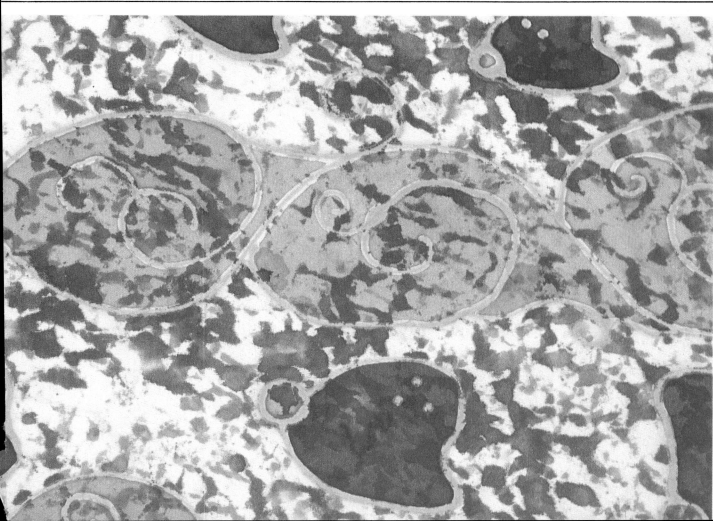

Preparing to Work

Every kind of technique in fabric painting requires that you spend some time in preparation, gathering your equipment together, preparing the fabric. This chapter is about frames, stretching the fabric in the frame and also gives guidelines about the best method of transferring designs to fabric

Some techniques require the cloth to be stretched taut in a frame. This makes it easier to work and also raises the fabric off the work surface, preventing smudging and increasing your efficiency. Tambour frames can be used or square or rectangular stretchers are obtainable from art suppliers (Fig 1). Old picture frames make ideal frames or you can make your own to suit your project.

Frames

Tambour frames
These frames come in several sizes and are available from most needle-work shops and departmental stores' haberdashery counters.

A tambour frame consists of two rings, one fitting inside the other. The fabric is placed over the smaller ring, then the larger is pressed down on top. The fabric is then pulled out round the frame so that the surface is taut, and a screw on the larger ring is tightened to hold the tension. Make sure the fabric

grain is straight and take care not to pull stretchy fabrics too tightly as the painted design could be distorted when the fabric is released from the frame.

Making a frame
Choose soft wood which is free from knots, about 12mm (½in) thick and 4.5–5cm (1¾–2in) wide. Soft wood enables pins to be inserted easily. If you are unsure of what to buy, ask the timber salesman to help you and explain exactly what the frame you are making is to be used for.

Decide the size and shape of the frame – square or rectangular – and have the wood cut to length. (For square frames, you will need 4 pieces of the same length. For a rectangular frame, you need 2 long pieces and 2 shorter pieces.)

Materials required
Sandpaper
4 pieces of soft wood cut to size
Wood glue
Geometric square
Tacks, hammer, or staples and gun
Beeswax

Fig 2 *Apply wood glue to the two surfaces then press together. Check the corner is square*

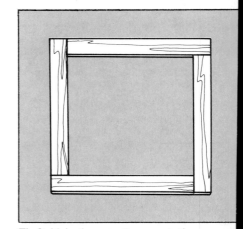

Fig 3 *Make the opposite corner in the same way, then glue both together. Leave to dry*

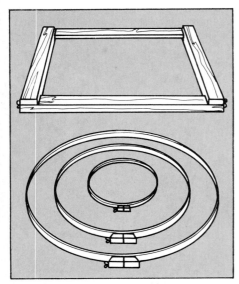

Fig 1 *Top: a square frame and (below) various sizes of embroidery tambour frames*

Fig 4 *Stretching fabric on a frame. Gently stretch and pin on opposite sides*

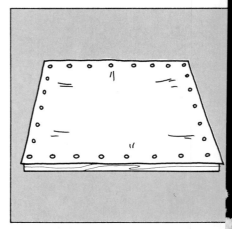

Fig 5 *Then gently stretch and pin the two remaining sides. The surface should be taut*

Method

Smooth the wood edges. Position 2 pieces on a work surface to make a square corner. Apply glue to the surfaces that touch, leave for a few seconds and then press the surfaces together (Fig 2). Check that the corner is square with the geometric square. Make the opposite corner in the same way and glue the two corners together (Fig 3). Leave to dry. Tack or staple to secure.

Polish with beeswax. This technique can be applied to any size of square or rectangular frame.

Stretching the fabric

Before starting, stretch the fabric tautly on a frame. The method for using tambour frames is described on the opposite page. On square or rectangular frames, the fabric is gently stretched and secured with three-pronged pins. These are best for the job as they do not snag the fabric. Spread the fabric across the frame and pin on opposite sides, starting in the middle (Fig 4). Adjust pins as required. Then pin the two remaining sides, adjusting the pins until the fabric is smooth and taut in the frame (Fig 5).

Masking tape Tape is an alternative to pins, but it works out more expensive because tape can rarely be used twice.

Once the fabric is stretched on the frame, you are ready to start painting.

Transferring designs

There are several ways of transferring designs onto fabric. Follow the method recommended for the particular technique.

Carbon transferring

Dressmakers' carbon sheets are used for transferring designs and marks onto fabric. Blue carbon paper is used for medium to light coloured fabrics, orange is best for light colours and white shows well on dark fabrics.

To use dressmaker's carbon paper, place the sheet, carbon side down, on the fabric. Place the design on top and trace the outline with a tracing wheel or blunt knitting needle (or similar tool).

Check that a good impression is being made by lifting one corner of the carbon paper. Only a faint outline is needed – the line can be painted over.

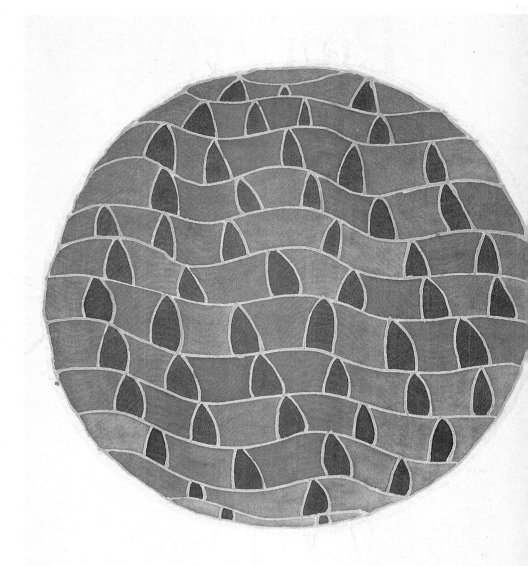

Pencil tracings

This simple technique requires a soft, drawing pencil (4b), and tracing paper. Ordinary grease-proof paper can be used but be careful as this tears easily.

Copy or draw the design directly on to tracing paper using the 4b pencil, making sure that the lines are well covered with pencil. Turn the tracing paper face down on the fabric and gently rub the outline into the cloth with the edge of a spoon or a coin. Lift a corner of the paper to check that the pencil is being transferred to the fabric. A faint outline is all that is needed. Retrace when the line cannot be seen.

Direct tracing method

If the fabric is sheer (and the painting technique suitable), the design can be

Above: Oriental Circle. Gold gutta resist with black and red, worked on Habotai silk

directly traced onto the cloth. Trace against a window pane or over a light box.

Draw your design on white paper, then, using a dark marker, emphasise the outline. Place the design underneath the fabric. Keeping the fabric absolutely flat and smooth (tape the fabric to the paper if necessary), trace the outline using a 4b soft pencil. Do not press too hard – only a faint outline is needed.

Trace markers

Some of these leave outlines on fabric which disappear within a few hours. Others vanish when water is applied.

Salt and Water Techniques

The use of salt and water in fabric painting is extremely popular both because of the simplicity of the methods – and because the finished effects can be breathtakingly beautiful

Salt technique
Materials and equipment

Fabrics
Fine textured, light-weight fabrics are used for this technique – Habotai, Antung, von-Shan, doupion and crépe de chine silks and sheer cottons (voilissima, primissima, cotton voile, lawn cotton and cambric). Nun's veiling produces the best effect in woollen fabrics.

Paint
The technique depends on a combination of fine fabric and runny paint. Use Deka silk, or a similar paint type.

Salt
The type of salt used determines the final effect. Fine grained kitchen salt is good for creating soft, washy backgrounds. Coarse sea salt produces more defined, striking effects.

Applicators
You will need pipettes, droppers or plastic straws for dripping the paint on to the fabric. Small, medium and large-sized brushes are used for marking lines and for covering large areas.

Preparation
Spray the fabric lightly with water. (Fig 1). Stretch the fabric on a frame. Use colours straight from the pots or decant into palettes.

Method
The effect depends largely upon the amount of paint and salt used, as the design is achieved through the interaction of fabric, paint and salt. This technique tends to work in mysterious ways, so the result can be a wonderful

Fig 1 *Spray the surface of the fabric very lightly with clean, cold water*

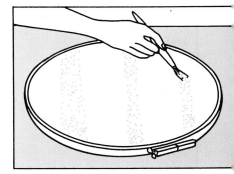

Fig 2 *Mount the fabric in a frame. Paint the light colours first, using a brush*

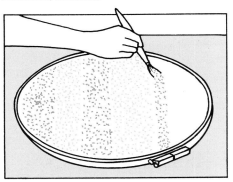

Fig 3 *Next, paint in the dark colours where they are required. Dilute paint if liked*

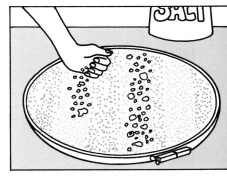

Fig 4 *Sprinkle salt on the wet paint, either all over or in specific areas, as required*

surprise.

Work out where you want the salt to achieve a 'crater' effect and then apply the paint. It will flow further and faster if diluted with water. Apply the light colours first (Fig 2).

Next, paint on the darker colours (Fig 3). While the paint is still wet, sprinkle the salt on the fabric as required (Fig 4).

Leave the salt and paint until completely dry, then brush off the salt with a clothes brush, or shake it off over a basin or newspaper.

(A hairdryer can be used to speed up the drying process, held beneath the

fabric and set at a low speed and medium heat.)

Fix the paints according to the manufacturer's instructions. If they are fixed by heat, rinse off the remaining salt with tepid water after the fabric has been ironed. (Steaming and fixing bath techniques dissolve the salt during the fixing process.)

Iron the fabric again and it is ready to be made up.

Right: free-flow paint with water added while paint is wet. Worked on Habotai silk and framed for window hangers

Water technique

The fabrics, paints and equipment used for the salt technique are also used here, except that water and alcohol are used instead of salt. The applicators are used not only for the paint, but also for the water, which must be kept clean and clear. The alcohol should be pure, or at least 80% proof.

Preparation
Prepare the fabric as for the salt technique, putting it into a frame.

Method
Cover all, or specific areas of the fabric with water and immediately apply the paint to achieve a very washy effect. As the paint and water flow into each other, light and dark shades will develop.

Diluting the water with a few drops of alcohol accentuates the effect and softens the brilliance of the paints.

Water can also be used to create lovely blob effects by dropping or painting water on to the fabric after it has been painted and while the colours are still very wet. The blobs spread, leaving detailed edge markings around soft washy centres. The dark pigments in the paint group together to form jagged veins, while the soft tones merge in a wash.

This technique lends itself to experimentation and you can build up a useful file of swatches with a detailed record of the colours and mixes used to create each effect.

Combined salt and water technique

The combination of both salt and water techniques creates fascinating designs. The materials and equipment are as for the salt technique.

Method
To achieve paint-run effects, apply paint to the fabric until it is so wet that small puddles are formed. The paint can either be used neat or diluted with water.

Stand the frame on end to make the paint run down the fabric. When it has almost reached the bottom, turn the frame 90° to make the paint change course and continue turning the frame until you are happy with the result. For extra effect, you could sprinkle salt, or drop water, onto the paint.

Designer tips 3

Ideas for effects When paints run together they create new colours so make sure the tones chosen make a complementary colour. It is a good idea to stick to a basic two or three colours. As the paints blend, the colour range increases automatically.

Salt and water designs can be further decorated by over-painting using brush strokes, printing or other techniques. Use only darker colours, however, as most of the paints used in this method are translucent and light paint will not show up over dark.

Above: free application painting in red, black, blue, green, yellow and pink on Habotai silks.
Right: Habotai silk cushion painted, using the salt and water technique.

Sponging

The sponging technique is very simple to work, but the results are exciting. Just one layer can be printed or several layers of colour can be built up, working from light to dark.

Materials and equipment

Fabric
Most fabrics are suitable for this technique and the result depends on the amount and type of paint used. Bleached cotton is ideal as it shows a clear print, but medium to heavy-weight silks also produce effective results.

Paint
Deka silk works well on heavier fabrics as the density of the cloth prevents the paint from spreading. Do not dilute with water and mix colours together neat to create new shades.

Deka permanent is suited to finer fabrics. If you want to increase the quantity of paint, add colourless Deka permanent, not water. Diluting with water thins the paint, and this should be avoided when fine fabric is being used.

Masking tape
Masking tape is used to block off areas that are not to be sponged. You can create stripes, lines, squares and diamond shapes with strips of tape.

Sponges
Use either natural or synthetic sponges.

Basic Technique

Preparation
Iron or press the fabric to remove any creases. Spread it over a thin layer of wadding. (This enables you to print using a gentle pressure.) Decant paints onto saucers so that the sponges can be dipped in easily. Use dry sponges, as any water in the sponges will dilute the paint and ruin the sponge print. If you are using masking tape, fix it to the fabric, making sure that the tape lies smooth (Fig 1).

Method
Dip the sponge lightly in the paint and remove excess paint by making the first print on a scrap of waste fabric. Now Paint the fabric, pressing then releasing the sponge gently (Fig 2)

Do not squeeze the sponge or press too hard. Experiment on a spare piece of cloth until you are confident of the results. Use a different sponge for each colour. Apply the next colour (Fig 3). Paint must be completely dry before another colour is applied unless you specifically want a smudged effect. Fix the paint.

Right: sponged designs on medium-weight cotton making use of masking tape for patterning

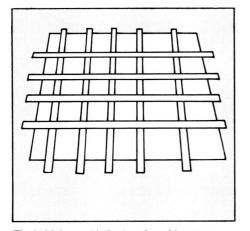

Fig 1 *Make a grid of strips of masking tape pressing it onto the fabric*

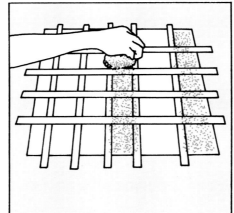

Fig 2 *Apply the first colours to certain areas using the sponge firmly but gently*

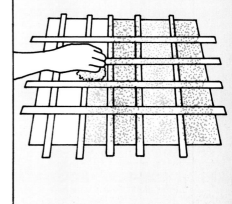

Fig 3 *Complete the design by applying the second colour in unpainted areas*

Uses for sponging

Sponging with fabric paint can be used to decorate fabric for all kinds of things for the home — towels and bed linens in particular are transformed by this very easy — and satisfying — method. Try designs and colour schemes on drawing paper first. Your experiments can be used afterwards to make attractive giftcards.

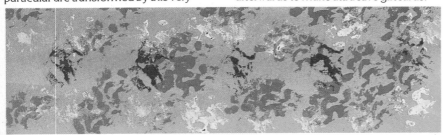

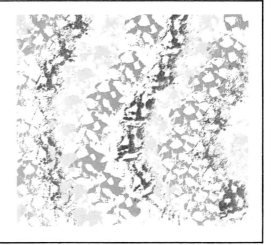

Rugs from Rags

During their long history of more than 2000 years, rag rugs have been used for a wide variety of purposes in the home – for bed covers and wall hangings and, sometimes, for warm clothing. This chapter shows how to make two different types of rag rug using fabric painting; a canvas-backed rug and a spiral-stitched rug.

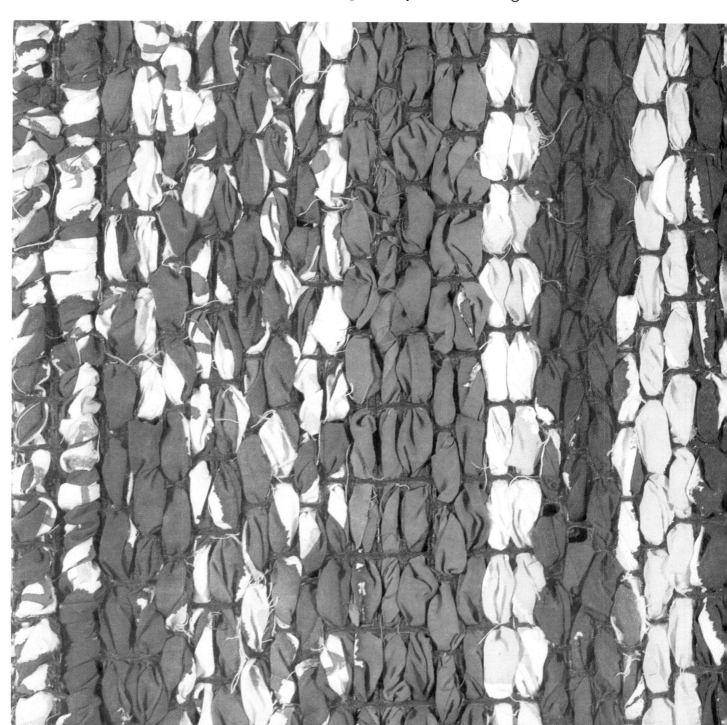

Canvas-backed rug

Materials and equipment required

Canvas
Choose an open-mesh canvas (rug canvas) with double threads and with 3–6 holes to 2.5cm (1in).

Needles
Large blunt darning or carpet needles with eyes large enough to take the fabric strips are needed for this method. Apart from turning over the ends of the strips and basting them into place, there is no real sewing involved. The fabric strips are secured by threading them through the holes in the canvas using a large-eyed needle.

To make this gay rug, the canvas was first painted red. Then strips of cotton painted yellow, red and blue were threaded through

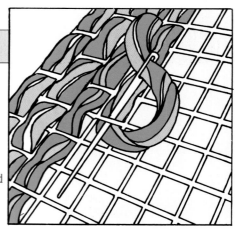

Fig 1 *Thread painted fabric strips through the canvas mesh using a large-eyed needle*

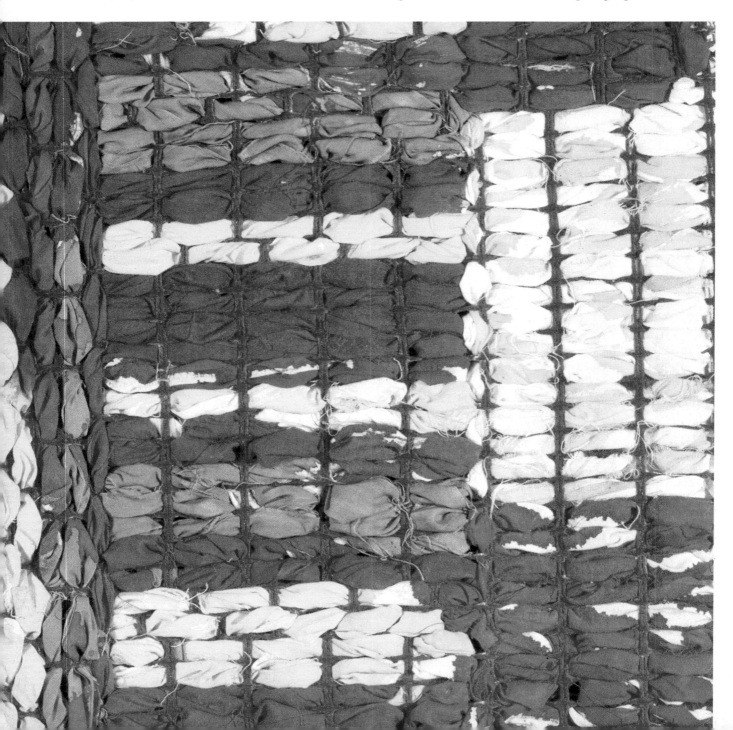

Canvas-backed rug designs

The patterns here can be worked to make canvas-backed rugs. Match the colours or choose schemes to match your own room furnishings. Experiment by threading the fabric strips through varying numbers of canvas threads.

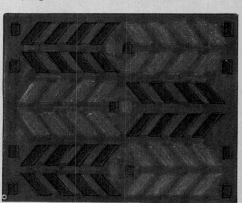

Preparation
Wash all the fabrics first in case of shrinkage.

Method
Paint the fabric and cut it into 5–7cm (2–2³⁄₄in)-wide strips. Thread the darning needle with one of the strips and weave it through the open-mesh canvas (Fig 1, page 19).

The rug is made even more effective if the canvas itself is painted in colours which match, or contrast, with the fabric strips.

Finish the project by turning the ends of the strips under the canvas and basting them down. Both braided and canvas rugs can be backed with felt or hessian to give a neater finish and make them last longer.

Braided rug

Materials required

Fabric
Choose a medium-weight cotton fabric such as bleached cotton or cotton drill. It must be hard-wearing as rugs get a lot of use. Make sure all the fabrics used are of similar weight, as uneven textures will make the rug lumpy and spoil the design.

Estimating quantities
For a 120cm (48in) finished length, allow an extra 50cm (20in) of plaiting. When coiling plaits, each round will take up about 20–22cm (8–8¹⁄₂in) more fabric than the preceding round.

Allow an extra 18–20cm (7¹⁄₄–8in) for joining strips together and for finishing the ends neatly.

Paint
Deka silk paints are suitable, but any paint of runny consistency would do, provided the colours spread into each other easily.

Fig 2 *Small spirals sewn to make a braided rug*

Preparation
Wash all the fabrics before using them in case of shrinkage.

Working the design
Any of the painting techniques described in this book can be used but remember that small, detailed designs will not show up when the rug is finished. Keep to simple methods, using the salt and water technique for extra effect, or experiment with sponging or paint spraying.

Apply the paint, leave it to dry, fix it and then iron or press the fabric to remove creases. You are now ready to cut it into strips. For a fine braid, cut strips about 6cm (2¹⁄₄in) wide which will allow for a 9mm (³⁄₈in) seam on either side. Double or even treble the width for a more chunky braid.

Cut the strips along the length of the fabric and machine-stitch them together to make 3–5m (3¹⁄₄–5¹⁄₂yd) lengths. Stitch the long edges together, wrong side out, to make tubes, and then turn them right side out again.

Braiding
Take three tube lengths of fabric and secure them at one end with a pin, or stitches. Put a heavy weight on this end and start plaiting. The weighted end enables you to maintain an even tension throughout the braid. When the plait is finished, turn the ends under and baste them. The braids can either be stitched or sewn together side by side to make a square rug, or coiled round to make a spiral rug. When coiling the plaits, make sure the stitches holding them are evenly spaced and of a consistent tension. There should not be any gaps or bumps.

Small spirals could also be made and sewn together to make a larger rug (Fig 2).

Paint spraying

Materials and equipment

Fabric
Any type of fabric is suitable but the amount of paint needed will vary with the weight of the cloth. A heavy fabric will need more paint than a medium or light-weight one.

Paint
This technique requires a thin, runny paint, applied either neat or diluted with water. Always make sure the paint is absolutely smooth, without any particles in it which could clog the spray nozzle. Pour the paint through a sieve if you are in any doubt.

Plant sprays
For background work, choose a spray with an adjustable nozzle capable of delivering a fine mist. A pump action is useful for a continuous flow of paint, but provided you keep up the tempo, an ordinary household or garden spray works perfectly well.

Spraying is a messy business so it is advisable to work outside on a dry, still day.

Basic technique

Preparation
Hang the fabric from a washing line rather than laying it flat on a work surface. Hanging helps the paint to spread evenly over the cloth.

Method
Move the spray rapidly over the fabric, producing as fine a mist as possible. The quicker you work, the more even the result will be (Fig 3).

The spraying method can be used in several ways. The fabric could be sponge-printed first in a dark colour, left to dry and then sprayed over in a light colour. Alternatively, spray the light one first and then follow up with a dark sponge print.

Plant sprays are useful for painting lining fabrics for rugs, curtains and wall hangings as well as for garments.

Fig 3 *Hang the fabric and spray paint evenly from about 30cm (12in) away*

Felt-tips and Crayons

Felt-tipped pens and wax crayons which have been specifically designed for fabric painting need very little additional equipment. They are non-toxic, clean to use and ideal for creating patterns on ready-made clothing, accessories and furnishings.

Materials and equipment

Fabrics

Most fabrics are suitable for pen and crayon decoration, but felt-tipped pen colours tend to run slightly on very fine or sheer fabrics. Try them out on a scrap of fabric before starting.

Fixing

Both pens and crayons are fixed by the heat method. The most effective way of fixing wax crayons is to put a piece of waste cloth on the ironing board and then place the design face down on top and iron the reverse side. This helps prevent the iron coming into direct contact with the wax.

Picnic set

Materials required

3m (3¹/₄yd) of medium to heavy-weight, white cotton
Felt-tip pens or wax crayons
Open basket with a handle, or a picnic basket with a lid

Preparation

Transfer the design to the fabric, or work freehand. The design can be drawn directly onto the fabric free-hand, but remember that these markers are permanent, even before the colours have been fixed. It's a good idea to have the design worked out carefully on paper first so that you know exactly where you are going to make your

marks. If the fabric is fairly thin, you m[?] be able to work over your paper desig[?] painting directly onto the fabric. Alternatively, use of any of the transferring methods described on page 11.

Working the design

Simple but very effective, the basket lining and table cloth and napkin desig[?] is based on small squares, made up of five horizontal and five vertical stripes. These are repeated until the fabric is covered. The outside of the basket is trimmed with a plait of three strips of striped fabric, woven through the open basket sides. The stripe is repeated as a[?] edging motif.

Lining the basket

Measure the inside of the basket, both base and sides, and add a 18mm (³/₄in) seam allowance all round. Add about 10cm (4in) to the length of the fabric used to cover the sides, for tucks so that the lining will fit snugly.

Machine-stitch the pieces of lining together and catch them to the basket with loose stitches. If the stitching is to[?] tight, the lining will pull out of shape. Cut the picnic cloth to 1.20m (48in) square and napkins to 30cm (12in) square. Press and machine-stitch doubled hems.

Top: two samples of colour blocking using felt-tipped pens. Below, an attractive set for a picnic made with ordinary white cotton sheeting and imaginative use of colour

Children's corner

Most children love working with paints and colours. Decorating textiles is particularly exciting, however, as the painted fabrics they produce can be made up into all kinds of usable things from school bags to clothes and bed linen. Felt-tipped pens and wax crayons are an ideal medium for them.

Although these paints are clean to use, it is important that children's clothes are protected with an apron as the pens leave permanent marks.

The kitchen table is usually the best work surface, provided it is well protected with an old cloth or newspapers. Let children experiment first on odd scraps of fabric. Then when they have found their artistic feet, they can decorate their plain white T-shirts, plimsolls or shorts. (Stick to felt-tips for plimsolls, as wax is almost impossible to fix on them.)

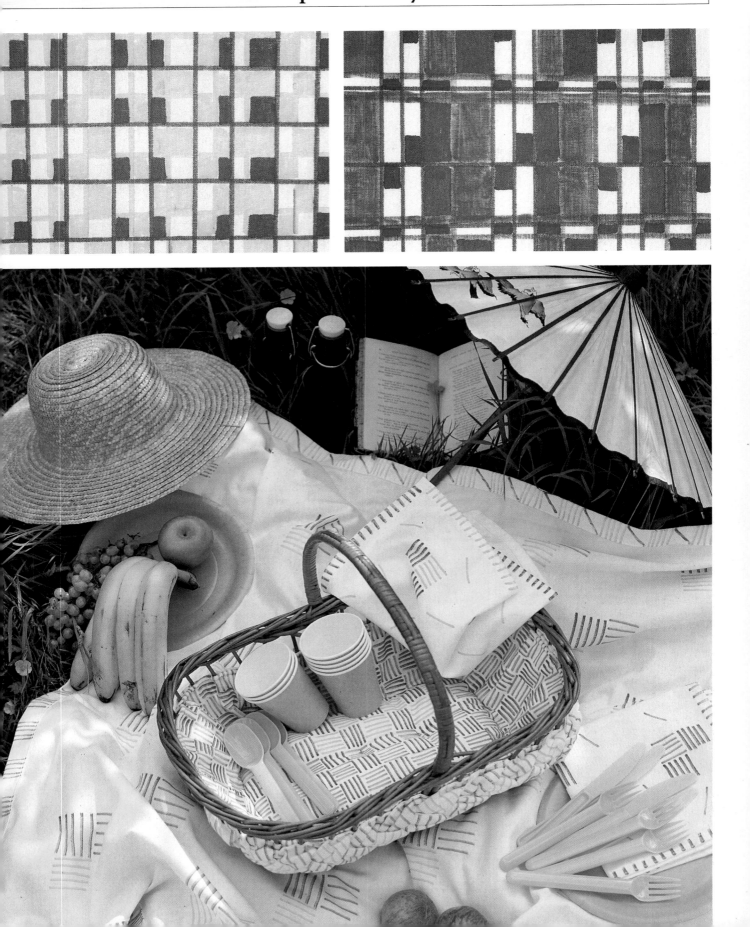

Stencilling

Stencilling has been used to decorate all kinds of surfaces for thousands of years — furniture, walls and ceramics — as well as textiles. The technique involves a 'mask' — the stencil — which has shapes cut into it. The stencil is placed on the fabric and paint is applied with a special brush within the cut-out design

The advantage of the stencilling technique in fabric printing is that the stencil can be used again and again to produce a repeat pattern.

Just one stencil can be used in a design, applying the colours to each cut-out area separately, or a picture can be built up using several different stencils, using one colour for each stencil application. This creates a much more intricate and varied design.

Materials and equipment

Fabrics
Apart from very sheer silk fabrics, almost any type of cloth is suitable.

For the towelling set, however, only one stencil is required. Wash it separately the first time after painting.

Paints
Stencil work requires paint of a fairly thick consistency to prevent the colours from running beneath the edge of the stencil and blurring the outline of your design.

Deka permanent paint is ideal but other paints of similar consistency can be used such as Dupont Imprefix 2. Spray paints sold in canisters are also excellent for stencilling. Spray paints can be obtained specially made for fabric, but matt car spray paints can also be used.

When using compressed sprays, always work in a well ventilated area to avoid any build-up of unpleasant fumes. Wear a protective face mask.

Applicators
Stencilling brushes have short, stubby bristles and come in several sizes. Choose a range that matches the areas of the stencil design.

Sponges can also be used for stencilling, giving a soft, mottled effect, as a contrast to the sharp defined outline produced by the stencilling brush.

Stencils
Ready-cut stencils can be obtained from most art and craft shops and come in a wide range of designs. They are very easy to use but building up a varied collection of designs can prove expensive. It is a good idea therefore to learn how to cut your own original stencils.

Cutting stencils
Traditionally, stencils are made of waxed paper. This is a medium thickness card which has been coated in linseed oil to prevent the stencil from soaking up the paint. Oiled paper may be difficult to find but it can usually be obtained from specialist arts and craft suppliers.

The most popular material for making stencils, however, is clear plastic. This material is easy to cut and, as the stencils are transparent, they can be positioned accurately on the fabric.

Plastic comes in A4–A1 sized sheets, but make sure the type you buy is not floppy. A limp stencil is difficult to position properly and may curl up at the edges.

Improvised blanks can be made by painting clear (or coloured) nail varnish along the cut edges of a simple cardbo stencil. To lengthen its life, further spra all over with clear varnish.

Cutting knives
Use a very sharp scalpel or Stanley knif for precision cutting. A scalpel is easies to work with.

Cutting surface
To protect your work surface, always cut stencils on a wooden chopping board or sheet of thick plastic sheeting Special cutting boards can be obtained from art suppliers.

Transferring designs
Typewriter carbon paper is used to transfer the design onto the stencil bla

Right: Navy bows on a pink, guest towel set. Below right, the same bow motif is also pretty for a baby

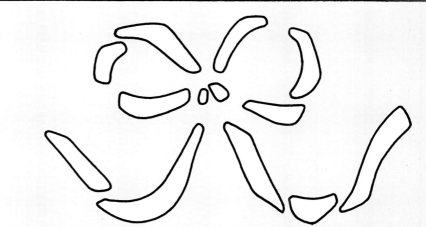

Use the ribbon motif for decorating bedroom curtains, perhaps making a matching pelmet and tiebacks. It might also be used to edge a dressing table skirt, or be worked around a soft lampshade

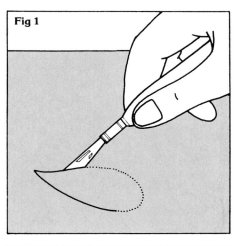

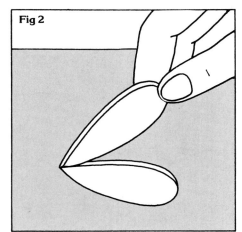

Teacup and teapot: sponging is used to create a soft, washed effect. Work this design as a picture or perhaps use it for a charming traycloth
Below: This simple two-colour tulip design could be used for curtain fabric, tablecloths, as a fashion fabric.

Fig 1 *Cutting a stencil: cut round the design line using a sharp scalpel point*

Fig 2 *Having cut round cleanly, the shape should lift away from the stencil blank easily*

Fig 3 *Paint the edges of card stencils with clear nail varnish to lengthen their life*

Fig 4 *Dab the loaded stencil brush on a piece of scrap paper or fabric to remove the excess paint*

Fig 5 *Apply the paint by dabbing the brush in an up and down movement, starting in the middle*

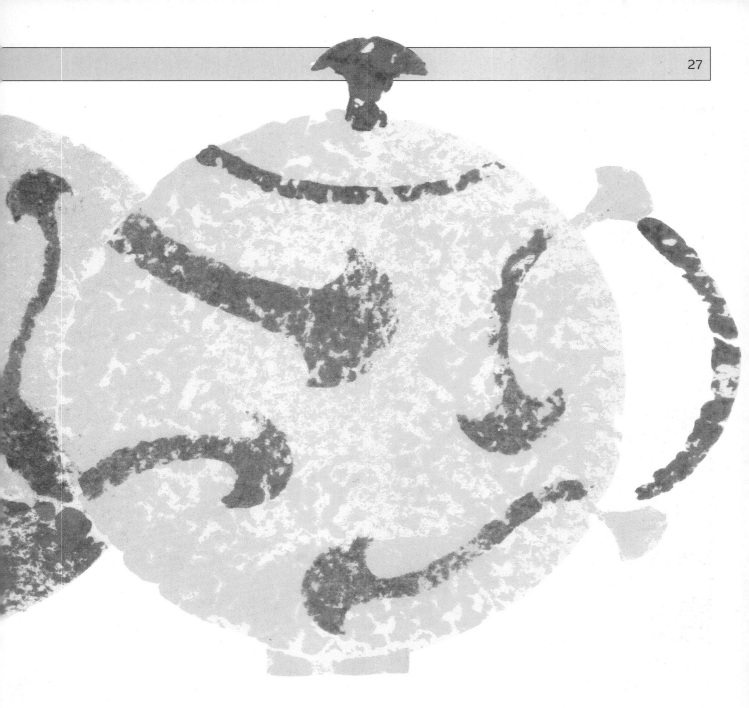

Basic technique

sing a scalpel, cut out the shapes,
naking sure that the outlines are
ccurate and the cut edges are smooth
nd even. (Rough edges interfere with
e smooth application of paint and
revent a clear reproduction of the
esign on the fabric.) See Fig 1.
emember to leave at least 3mm *(¹/₈in)*
etween cut-out shapes. Lift out the
ut-out pieces and discard (Fig 2). Nail
arnish can be painted on the edges of
aper stencils to extend their useful life
Fig 3).

If the design you want is very intricate

or complicated, you will need to cut
several stencils, one for each colour, to
build up the picture.

Preparation

Lay the stencil on the right side of the
fabric and secure it with masking tape
to prevent the stencil from moving
while you work.

Working the design

Dip the brush (or applicator) in the paint
and test it on a scrap of paper or fabric.
This also helps to remove excess paint
(Fig 4). Apply the paint with a dabbing
motion to obtain an even covering.
(A shaded effect can be created by

applying more paint on one edge than
the other.)

Always work from the centre out
(Fig 5), taking care not to flood the fabric
with paint as it could seep under the
stencil and spoil the design. Paint all the
cut-out areas of the stencil and leave for
a few minutes before lifting the stencil
carefully from the fabric.

Clean the stencil on both sides to
remove all the paint, and then tape it
down again for the next application. If
you are working with several stencils
placed one on top of the other, make
quite sure that the paint from the
previous application is completely dry,
to prevent smudging.

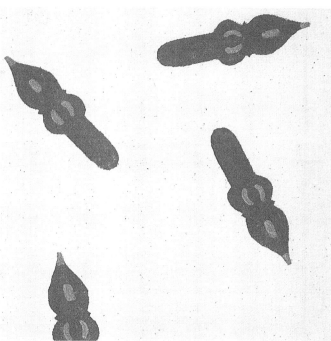

Top left: Desert Rose.
Careful cutting is required
for this pretty motif. It could
be used for table linens, bed
linens or perhaps for the
pocket of a blouse or dress

Above: Blue Ink. Gold paint
has been used for extra
effect in this design, which
would make an attractive
fabric for a small school
bag or tote bag

Left: Trumpet Narcissi. This
graceful design is not too
difficult to cut out and
would be suitable for
applying to table linen, or
might decorate a complete
bathroom set

Drawing on and Painting in

This simple technique dates back thousands of years. The outline of the design is drawn onto the fabric first, paint is then applied within the lines using a brush. The method gives considerable scope for experimentation

Ship ahoy dress

This pinafore dress has been made using a commercial paper pattern. Voilissima was used but other fabrics would work equally well such as cambric, lawn, primissima, cotton voile or a crisp cotton.

If you are using a light-weight fabric, the dress should be lined.

Paint

This technique requires paints with a thick, non-runny consistency. Deka permanent has been used for the dress pictured but any paint that does not spread would be suitable. Do not dilute the paint with water because the water often separates from the pigment when the fabric is painted, leaving streaks and smudges of colour.

Mix the colours together neat, and take care to blend them thoroughly. Gritty bits can be removed by straining the paint through a sieve.

Preparation

Cut out the garment pieces. Trace the designs (Fig 1) and transfer onto the fabric before making up the garment. Refer to the picture for the arrangement.

Working the design

Paint in the pattern, following (Fig 1) taking care to keep within the outlines. The paint should be applied smoothly and cover the fabric evenly.

The hem ruffle, the collar and the shoulder insets were painted free-hand with a small wave motif and a dot pattern. Use the tip of a pointed brush for the dots and waves.

Finishing

Fix the paints following the manufacturer's instructions. Make up the garment as instructed in the pattern.

The simple sailing boat, waves and air bubbles motifs (Fig 1) make a charming decoration for a little girl's dress or smock. Painted on fine white cotton, a nostalgic, 1900's look is achieved. The motifs might be repeated on a pair of beach shoes (see page 64)

Fig 1

Kingfishers

This inspiring picture of water lilies and a pair of kingfishers was designed by the author. If you would like to reproduce this, trace the picture from the page and then transfer it to fabric using any of the techniques described on page 11. Pearlised paints are used for a shimmering effect.

Marbling

Marbling of paper is an ancient craft first developed around 1,500 years ago. In this chaper, the basic technique is used to produce beautiful painted fabrics. The possibilities are almost endless.

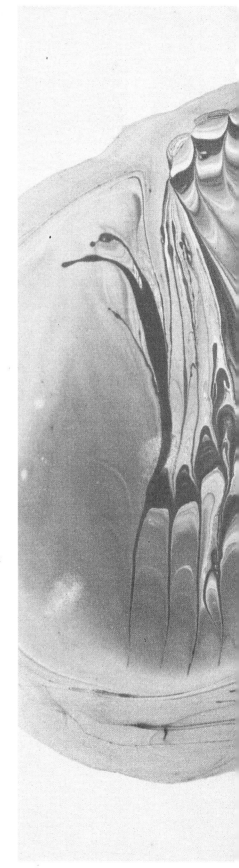

The technique of marbling is simple, although the results can be spectacular. It requires a base fluid, made from water mixed with a thickener such as wall-paper paste or seaweed. Paints are then dropped onto the base with a pipette, eye-dropper or a special drop brush.

When the paint is floating on the base, patterns are created by pulling the paint to and fro with comb-like tools to create the typical marbling swirls.

The fabric (or paper) is then laid on the floating paint. When the fabric (or paper) is lifted, the paint pattern has been transferred to the material.

A fresh paint pattern has to be created on the base every time a transfer is made.

Materials and equipment

Fabric
Most plain fabrics are suitable for marbling. Cotton, silk and wool are particularly effective, but man-made fibres can be used as well.

Paint
Oil-based paints are used, being easily floated on the base and they hold the pattern steady while being transferred to the fabric.

Experiment with your chosen paints before embarking on a major project because some do not need a base thickener as they float on the miniscus of the water without sinking. Most paints, however, need a well-thickened base.

Fabric paints can be used as an alternative to oil paints, but the base needs to be slightly thicker in consistency to enable the light fabric paints to float. You will need to spend some time experimenting with these also as they are trickier to handle than oil paints. Two or three hours will be enough to familiarise yourself with the technique of making a base and floating fabric paint colours on top.

Deka silk and Deka permanent paints have been used for the samples pictured.

Applicators
Pipettes and eye-droppers are the best tools for directing controlled drops of paint onto the base. Always use a different dropper for each colour. Drop brushes are also suitable, but the amount of paint in the dropper will vary according to the size and capacity of the brush. They are particularly useful when you want to create larger splashes of colour.

Patterning tools
A variety of tools can be used to create patterns in the paint, but the most popular are ordinary hair combs. These can be as short in length or as wide as the tray containing the base fluid – the size depends entirely on the effect you want to achieve. Wide-toothed combs made of metal or plastic can be bought almost everywhere – or you can make your own. Hammer nails through pieces of wood (the spaces between the nails can be varied – see Fig1 to Fig4 on page 36).

Children's toy garden rakes, kitchen knives, wooden sticks, knitting needles and large bird's feathers can all be used to create patterns.

Trays
Strong plastic dishes or trays are required to hold the thick base on which the paints are floated. They should be about 8cm *(3¹/₄in)* deep and are available from art, photographic and photographic materials suppliers.

As an alternative, you might use plastic seed trays as long as they do not have holes punched in the base.

Pet litter trays can be bought and these are quite large sized so they can be utilized as marbling trays

Beautifully marbled piece of creamy Antung silk which might be framed for a picture

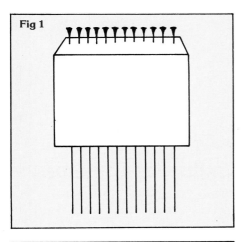

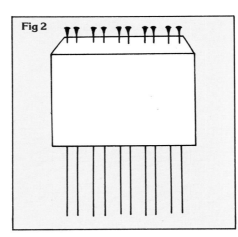

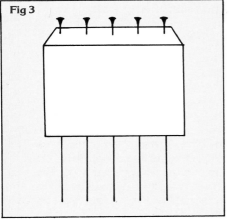

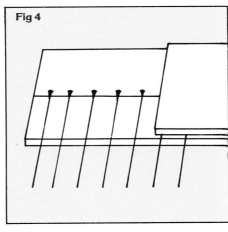

Old newspaper

You will need lots of old newspaper for this technique. Paper will protect the work surface and also provide somewhere for the wet painted fabric to rest while drying. Hanging marbled fabric to dry is not recommended as the paint could run down the cloth and distort the design.

Marbling bases

The consistency of the base is crucial to the success of the marbling. Various thickening agents can be used. Wallpaper paste, seaweed and carrageen moss are all suitable and other thickeners can be found in art and craft shops.

As the base is so important in marbling, spend time perfecting the skill of base-making.

Fig 1 *Long nails equidistantly spaced*

Fig 2 *Nails in groups of two spaced apart*

Fig 3 *Wide spaces set between long nails*

Fig 4 *Pins sandwiched between card layers*

All the marbling samples here were designed by the author and mounted for greetings cards

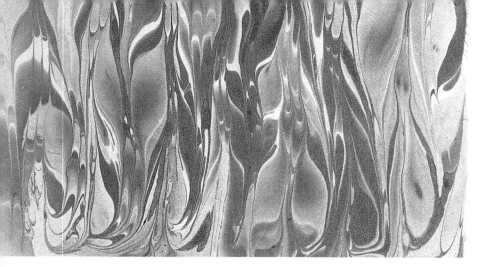

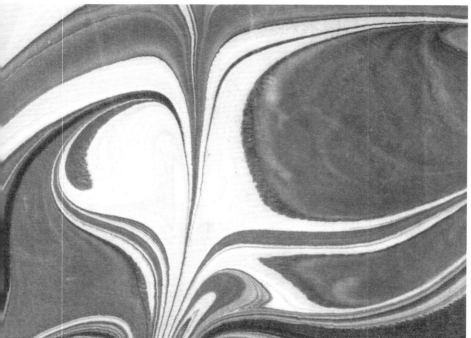

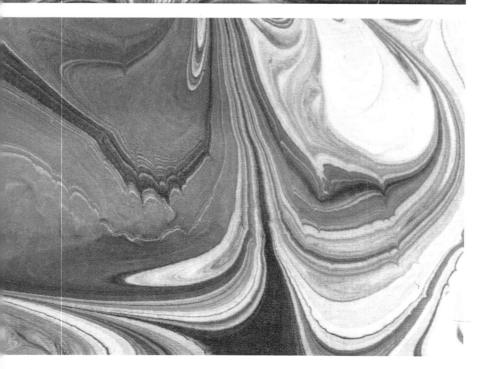

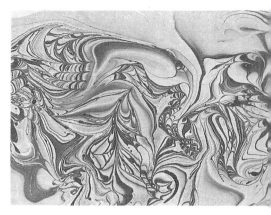

Wallpaper paste base

Materials and equipment

1 litre (1³/₄pt) lukewarm water
50g (2oz) wallpaper paste powder
Large container for mixing
Hand whisk
Strainer or sieve
A plastic tray for marbling

Method

Pour the luke warm water into the container and gradually sprinkling in the paste powder, begin whisking. As the powder dissolves, add more, whisking all the time to prevent lumps forming. Aim for a consistency like thick custard. If lumps do form, pour the mixture through a sieve before transferring it to the marbling tray.

Pour it into the tray and leave to stand for about 30 minutes before using.

Seaweed base

Seaweed and algae are good for the technique. Seaweed products designed specially for marbling can be found in most art and craft shops, but the process of making a seaweed base is quite different from the previous method described and requires great care.

Materials and equipment

250g (9oz) seaweed
1 litre (1³/₄pt) water. (If the water is particularly hard, add 100g (4oz) of borax before putting in the seaweed)
Wooden spoon
Sieve or strainer
Marbling tray

Method

Mix the seaweed powder with water and heat, according to manufacturer's instructions, stirring well until the mixture thickens. Remove pan from heat and force the mixture through a seive or strainer. Pour the thick, clear base into the marbling tray and leave to set. It is then ready for use.

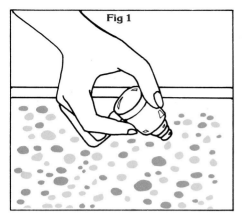

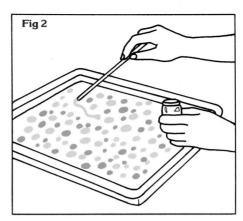

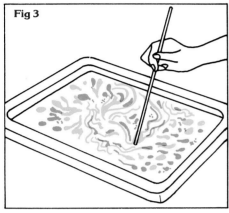

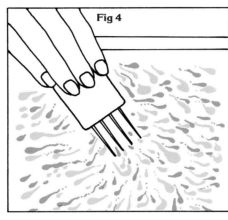

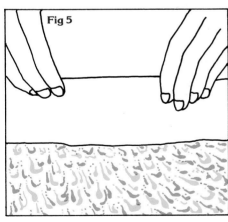

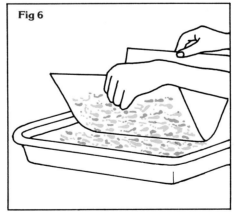

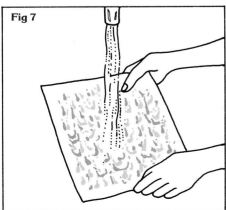

Fig 1 *Dropping paint onto base with a paint dispenser bottle*

Fig 2 *Dropping paint onto the base using an ordinary wooden stick*

Fig 3 *A single implement is used to pull paint in different directions*

Fig 4 *A four-pronged instrument, such as nails in wood, for a structured design*

Fig 5 *Lift the fabric by two corners and gently lay it on the top of the paint*

Fig 6 *Lift the fabric off the base carefully. The design will have transferred*

Fig 7 *Rinse the printed fabric under cold, running water, spread to dry*

Basic technique

Preparation
Cover the work surface with newspaper Prepare the base material. The fabric being used should have been washed and pressed. Washing dissolves any finishes which would repel the paint.

Method
Begin with just two or three colours, decanted into small liqueur-type glasses. This makes it easier for you to fill an eye-dropper or load a brush.

Hold the applicator over the base, taking care not to touch it. Apply the paint drop by drop in any pattern you like until almost the entire surface of the base has been covered with paint (Figs and 2). Vary the amount of paint to achie the base, you are ready to pull the colours and create the marbling.

Every attempt at marbling will achieve something different, but the kind of tool used will dictate the broad type of pattern created.

Single sticks (Fig 3) or short combs (Fig 4) can be used to pull the paint into swirling patterns, while long combs will give a more streaked effect. Pull the colours until a satisfactory design has been reached.

Lift the fabric by two corners and lay it down gently on the paint (Fig 5). Using a little pressure of the palm of the hand, smooth the cloth until it is lying completely flat on the base tray. Take care not to press so hard that the paint is forced down into the base gel.

Now lift the fabric off the base very carefully (Fig 6). You will find the pattern has cleanly transferred onto the fabric. Any paint left behind on the base tray can be used to create a lighter copy of the design on another piece of fabric. Remember to renew the base when you introduce different colours.

Rinse the printed fabric under runnin water to remove traces of base and lay it on old newspaper to dry (Fig 7)

Above: Leather and marbled silk have been worked into a patchwork and used to create this striking wall hanging
Right: Opera. By framing pieces of marbled fabrics a moving picture is created. In this design, by the author, small pieces of fabric are folded, pleated and knotted, and help to make the frame part of the picture

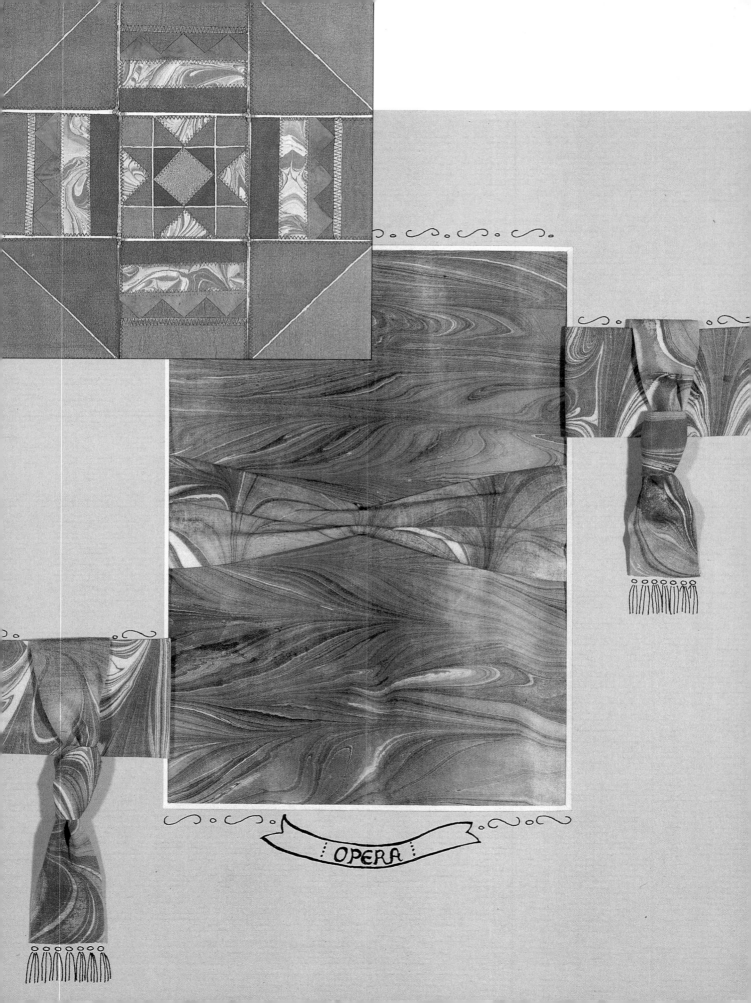

OPERA

Batik

The ancient art of batik was first practised by the Indonesians of Java and Bali, who painted religious and cultural scenes on fabric to create a historical record of island life. Batik is now a popular technique, used worldwide for decorating fabrics for clothing and upholstery.

Batik uses hot wax drawn or painted on fabric, either to act as a barrier to the spread of paint or dye, or to create patterns of hairline cracks for the paint to seep into.

Drawing outlines in hot wax is called 'cerne'. Paint is applied within the wax outline which stops the colours from running. When the wax is removed, the design should have a clear definition.

To create the characteristic batik cracked effect, brittle wax is spread onto the fabric with a brush. When it is dry, this wax skin is crumpled so that it is covered in hairline cracks. The fabric is then dipped or painted and the paint stains through the cracks.

Materials and equipment

Fabric
Any type of light-weight cotton or silk is suitable for batik, though the traditional fabric used is primissima, a very smooth, soft and delicate cotton which holds both wax and paint very well.

Paint
Special batik dyes are available in the Deka L series. These come in powder form together with a fixing bath. Dylon cold water dyes are also suitable.

A number of paints supplied by art and craft shops are specified as being for batik, but check that they are specifically designed for the hot wax technique before purchasing.

Below: Tulips. The design is worked in lilacs and pinks on a shantung dupion silk. Right: detail of a large batik shawl

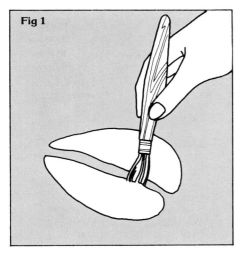

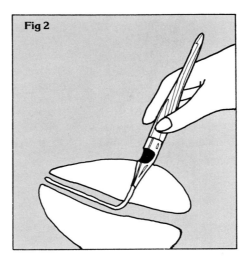

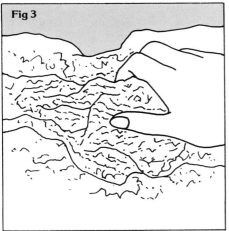

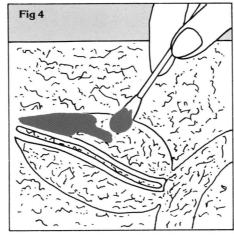

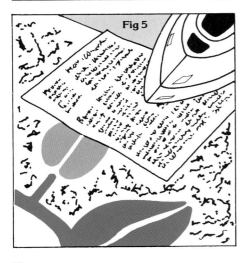

Fig 1 *Work melted wax on to the large areas of the design, using a brush*

Fig 2 *Draw in lines using melted wax in a tjanting*

Fig 3 *Crush the waxed fabric in your hand for a crackle effect*

Fig 4 *Drag a paint-dipped cotton wool bud over the cracks in the wax*

Fig 5 *To remove wax, cover the batik with old newspaper and iron, repeat as necessary*

Melting the wax

This part of the batik process requires extreme care. Keep children well clear of the hot wax. Wax should never be heated over a naked flame. A small, electric ring is ideal, or use a domestic electric cooker.

Specially designed wax melting pots are available or use a deep aluminium cooking pan or saucepan.

Wax melting pots have their own heating unit incorporated, designed to keep the wax at an even temperature. This means that the wax does not have to be constantly reheated, as would be the case with an electric ring and saucepan.

Fill the pan half-full with wax. Never fill it to the top. Increase the heat gradually, so that the wax melts slowly. Remember that all wax is flammable but brittle wax needs particular care because of its high paraffin content. The greater the proportion of paraffin, the more flammable the wax.

Never leave the wax while it is being melted. Just turning your back for a second can result in a burnt-out room, so watch the pot all the time. As soon as the wax becomes a clear, golden liquid remove it from the stove (unless you are using a proper melting pot).

If the wax begins to give off black fumes, take it off the heat immediately as the fumes are also highly flammable. Because of the dangers inherent in heating wax, make sure you are not going to be disturbed. Ignore telephones and doorbells: ask someone else to answer them, and keep children well away from the hot wax while it is being melted.

Applicators
Brushes

Brushes are ideal for beginners learning how to work in hot wax, as the wax is simply painted onto the fabric (Fig 1). The best brushes for batik are those with man-made fibre bristles as they last longer than the more expensive natural fibre bristles.

Tjanting

This is one of the traditional Indonesian tools used to work the batik technique. It consists of a copper bowl with a spout, set on a wooden handle.

Left to right: A wax melting pot, half-filled with wax granules, tjap, cotton wool buds, tjanting brushes and batik powder colours

Frames

A frame is essential for batik to lift the fabric up off the work surface. Any contact between wax or paint and the work top will spoil your efforts.

Wax

This is the most vital ingredient in batik. It comes as candles, blocks or granules, but the form is unimportant: what matters is the consistency.

Wax used for drawing needs to be of different consistency from wax used for cracking, (known as brittle wax). As the word brittle implies, this wax is too weak to be used as a barrier.

Drawing wax should be 40% beeswax and 60% paraffin wax. Brittle wax is 30% beeswax and 70% paraffin wax.

Tjantings are available from crafts and art shops and come in various sizes.

The tjanting is dipped in the hot wax and left in the pot for a few seconds to bring the copper bowl to the same temperature as the wax. If the bowl is cold, it will rapidly cool the wax and prevent you from working smoothly and continuously. When the bowl is hot and full of wax, remove it from the pot. The hot wax will run from the spout onto the cloth in a steady flow. Hold the tjanting just a little above the fabric and move your hand so that the flow of wax is directed along the design line (Fig 2). Have a small piece of scrap fabric ready to block the end of the spout when you have finished drawing. When the wax is set and dry, paint is applied within the wax barriers.

Tjap

This traditional tool is used for printing wax designs onto fabric. It consists of a wire base, on which fine strips of copper have been soldered, with a wooden pressing handle. The copper strips are bent into a design, usually of flowers and leaves. Tjaps are not easy to find but if you are serious about batik, try to obtain one.

To use a tjap, pour the melted wax into a metal or aluminium tray wide enough to take the tool. Immerse it in the wax and leave it for a few seconds for the copper wire to reach the same temperature as the wax, (as with the tjanting method).

Remove the tjap from the tray and let the excess wax drip off. Now bring the tjap to the fabric, position it and press the tjap down onto the cloth in one movement. Maintain the pressure for a few seconds and then lift off the tjap. You should be left with a clear wax print of the tjap design on the fabric. Leave the wax to dry and paint between the outlines with a brush.

Transferring designs

If you have a steady hand and a confident eye, apply the wax directly onto the fabric without marking out the design first. For a specific design, however, it is better to transfer the lines using the direct tracing technique. Until you are more experienced, keep to simple designs and outlines. You will find that even these produce very attractive results.

The cracking method

For this technique, brittle wax is painted over the area where the cracked effect is wanted, using a brush (Fig 1, page 42). Leave the wax to dry completely and then lightly crumple the fabric between your fingers (Fig 3). The wax will crack immediately. Spread out the fabric and apply paint with a brush or a cotton wool bud (Fig 4). Or immerse the fabric in a dye dip bath. The brush or cotton wool bud is dipped into paint and wiped up and down the cracked wax.

If a dye bath is being use, immerse the fabric until it is soaked in paint. Lift it out and hang to dry before fixing the colours.

Removing the wax

When you have finished applying both wax and paint and the fabric is fixed and dried, you are ready to remove the wax coating.

Place the fabric, wax side up, on a protective layer of newspaper (or on an old bed sheet) on a flat surface. Cover the wax with a single sheet of newspaper. Set an electric iron to the correct setting for the fabric and iron over the paper. As soon as it begins to absorb the melted wax, replace it with fresh sheet and continue with fresh

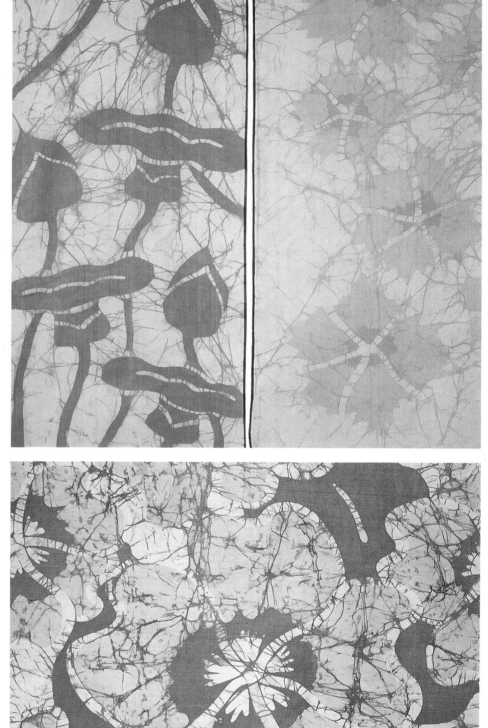

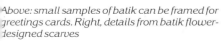

Above: small samples of batik can be framed for greetings cards. Right, details from batik flower-designed scarves

sheets until all the wax has been lifted off the fabric (Fig 5).

Ironing off the wax is probably the most laborious part of the batik process, but it is important to do it carefully. Then wash the fabric in hot soapy water to remove any residue of wax.

Gutta and Serti

The terms gutta and serti both refer to a barrier technique which is a modern version of the ancient batik method. Gutta is a German product and serti a French but as gutta is easier for beginners to handle, this product is used for projects in this chapter.

Working on the same principle as batik wax, gutta and serti liquids are applied to fabric and act as a barrier to stop the spread of paint. Unlike wax, however, neither product can be used for the veined cracking effect, but they have the advantage of being much easier to work with.

The two barrier materials are made up of quite different ingredients and are removed from fabric in different ways.

Gutta is removed using a mild soap and water solution and is fixed by ironing. Serti is removed by dipping the painted fabric in a bath of white spirit after steam fixing.

Materials and equipment

Paints

The paints used with gutta (and serti) need to be of a fairly runny consistency to enable them to spread rapidly across the fabric. Make sure the paint used is compatible with the barrier fluid. Deka silk is ideal for water-soluble gutta. Dupont and Pebeo Orient silk paints are used with the French serti barrier.

Applicators
Gutta pen

The most effective – and easiest – way of applying gutta is with a specially designed metal pen (see Fig 2) attached to a pipette bottle filled with the liquid (see bottle in Fig 1).

The tip of the bottle is snipped off (Fig 2) and the metal pen slipped into the spout. The pen is kept in place with masking tape (Fig 3). Ordinary clear adhesive tape will not do as it lets the fluid run out. The gutta bottle is squeezed and the fluid runs onto the fabric through a fine steel tube at the end of the pen (Fig 4). These pens are usually sold with a fine copper wire pushed up inside. Always

replace the wire inside the pen when you have finished using it to prevent the gutta makes drying in the pen nib. Dried gutta it impossible for the pen to work properly.

Fabrics

A wide range of fabrics can be used with the gutta and serti techniques. Light-weight silks such as Habotai, crêpe de chine and Antung silks are the most popular together with silks of similar weight and texture.

Light-weight cottons such as cambric, voilissima, cotton voile, fine lawn, primissima and other cottons of similar weight and texture are suitable also. The only drawback with cotton is that the clear barrier fluid is hard to see without shining a light on it, either from above or below, to illuminate the transparent outlines. Coloured gutta and serti work perfectly well on cotton as they show up. Wool fabric, such as fine lambswool nun's veiling can be used but again like cotton, the barrier outlines may be difficult to see. Thick or rough texture fabrics are not so good for these techniques because the barrier fluids cannot penetrate the fibres. Some fabric finishing processes may also prevent the barrier fluid from being absorbed properly. If the fabric you are proposing to use appears to have been treated, wash it thoroughly first.

Right: The centre of the cushion is a salt wash creating the illusion of a profusion of flowers. The butterflies at the corners are worked from the trace-off pattern on page 50 in black gutta and pink, gold and blue paint. Note that the whole of the trailing butterfly wing is used for this design

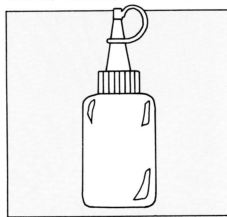

Fig 1 *Squeeze bottle of gutta barrier fluid with cap on the spout*

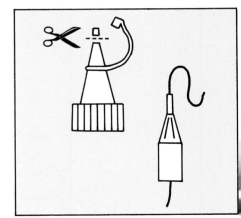

Fig 2 *Snip the top from the spout with scissors. The metal pen is shown*

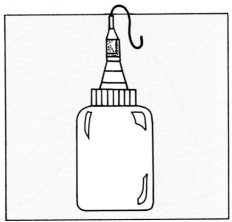

Fig 3 *Slip the metal pen into the cut spout and secure with masking tape*

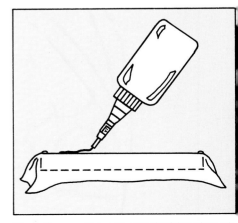

Fig 4 *Squeeze the gutta onto the fabric through the tube at the end of the pen*

Frames

The fabric needs to be smooth and taut for the gutta technique to succeed, so framing your work is essential.

Basic technique

Preparation

Stretch the fabric in a frame, making sure there are no dips or ridges when the palm of the hand is run over the surface.

Method

The term 'gutta' will be used to cover both barrier fluids.

Take hold of the pen and gutta bottle as you would an ordinary pen or brush. Try out the pen on a piece of paper first to make sure the fluid is running free before drawing on the fabric. As you draw, squeeze the bottle (Fig 1 page 50). This may seem difficult at first but once you have mastered the two actions, you will find the technique quite easy.

When the gutta outline is completed, hold the fabric to the light to check for gaps in the lines (Fig 2). Fill with more gutta, as it is vital there are no breaks in the outlines. Breaks will let the paint seep through and spoil the design.

Leave the gutta to dry naturally (or you can speed up the process with a hand-held blow dryer, set at medium heat and speed). Do not attempt to paint the fabric while the gutta is still wet unless you are very confident that you will not foul the gutta lines with the paint applicator.

Painting the fabric is straightforward. Apply the paint with a brush or a cotton wool bud, taking care to keep within the line. Use a fine brush for the corners and wider for broad areas. The important thing is to work steadily and fairly fast in order to avoid any streaking of the paint. Sometimes, however, you may want streaking as a deliberate effect.

Wait until all the paint is dry and then remove the fabric from the frame and fix it, following the method recommended for the paint and barrier material.

Other techniques

Gutta can be used in combination with salt and water techniques (see page

An evening bag of Antung silk which has been painted in a free-flow technique in sienna, ochre and blue. The fabric is patchworked, then embroidered and quilted. Twisted strips of fabric are applied to the bag flap

). However, be careful not to soak the
fabric with water as it could dissolve the
water-soluble gutta outlines.
If things go wrong, with paint seeping

through the gutta barriers, the salt
technique can be used to distract from
the mistakes. Do not despair if a project
does not succeed first time. Keep

trying, and you will find that it gets
easier all the time.

The flower and tendrils spray
is used on the front of a T-sha~
shirt worn under the kimono
(see small inset picture belou~

Fig 1 Hold the gutta bottle and pen as you
would an ordinary pen or brush

Fig 2 Hold the outlined design to the
light to check for gaps in the line

Left: Trace-off pattern
for the butterfly desig~
used on the kimono
(right), the cushion o~
pages 47 and 52, an~
the sculptured butter~
on the book cover ar~
on page 53. The long~
upper wing is omitte~
for the kimono and th~
book cover butterflies
Right: detail shows th~
shirt worn under the
kimono with flower
and tendrils spray m~

Butterfly collection

Use the pretty butterfly trace-off design opposite to decorate a kimono, a cushion and a book cover.

Kimono

Materials and equipment required

Fabric The kimono is made of crêpe de chine and lined with 8mm *(1/3in)* habotai silk.

Paint and barrier Deka Silk, transparent; water soluble gutta.

Frames Tambour frames of varying sizes will be needed to avoid having to stick pins in the delicate crêpe de chine. A large frame, usually used for quilting, will enable the butterflies design on the back of the kimono to be painted in one go. The other butterflies can be painted separately, stretched on smaller frames.

Kimono pattern

Use a commercial paper pattern for a kimono, which can be found in most pattern collections.

Preparation

Cut out the garment pieces. Work the design before making up. Transfer the butterfly motifs to the garment pieces using the direct tracing method.

Working the design

Draw along the outlines of the butterflies using gutta and pen. Paint in the colours, following the picture. Paint the stripes on the neckband and sleeve bands directly onto the fabric. Space the stripes to avoid the colours running into each other.

Finishing

Fix the paints. Make up the kimono according to the pattern instructions.

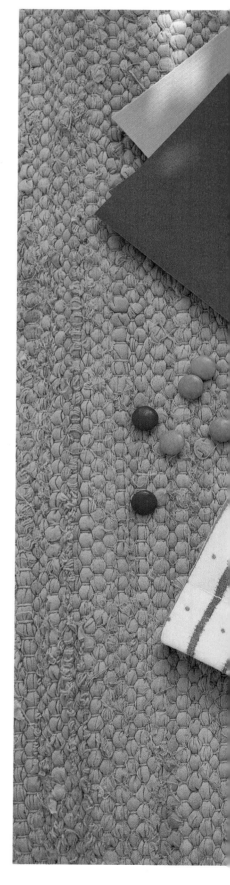

Butterfly cushion

This attractive silk cushion was designed using black gutta in combination with the salt method. The cream coloured silk has softened the effect of the colour.

Materials required

Fabric: Antung ivory silk
Paint and barrier: Deka Silk, black gutta

Preparation
Cut the cushion back and front to size. Draw the design on the right side of the cushion front using light pencil lines. Mount the fabric in a frame.

Working the design
Draw along the pencilled lines using black gutta in the pen. When the butterflies have been painted in, apply the salt technique. While the salt is doing its work, add small drops of water to the salt patches to give a washy, watercolour effect.

Finishing
Fix the paints and remove the salt. (The black gutta lines are not removed as they are part of the design and are fixed with the paint.)

Right: The book cover is painted in yellow, red and blue stripes and then two fabric sculpture butterflies are sewn to the cover. This idea might be developed with other designs, flowers or leaves, or fish forms would be suitable shapes for the sculpture method

Book cover

This unusual book cover is made up using a soft sculpture technique. The butterflies were painted on the fabric using the gutta process. The shapes were then cut out and the backing cut from fabric to the same shape. Placed right sides together, the shapes were sewn together all round, leaving a gap for filling. After turning right side out, the butterflies were filled and the sewing completed. The bodies were also stitched to give better definition to the wings. The padded butterflies were then sewn on to a background fabric painted in simple stripes with gold gutta dots, echoing the colours in the butterflies. Gold gutta is also used to paint the butterflies' antennae on the background fabric.

This type of sculpture can be used in many different ways. Flower and leaf designs are also effective and the technique is ideal for making children's mobiles.

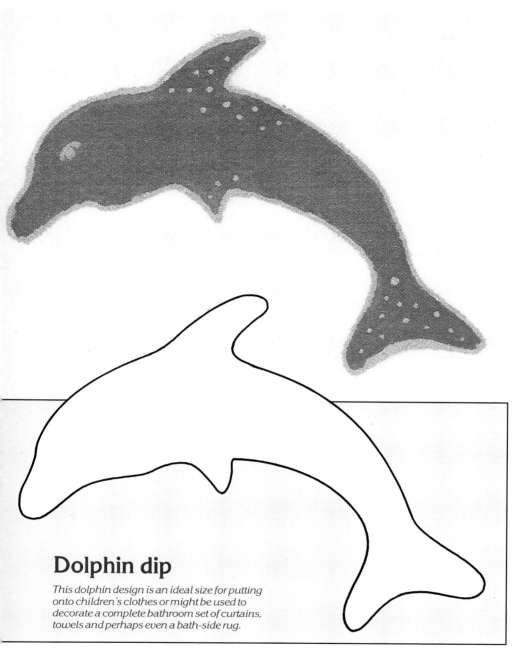

Dolphin dip

This dolphin design is an ideal size for putting onto children's clothes or might be used to decorate a complete bathroom set of curtains, towels and perhaps even a bath-side rug.

Tulip time

The beautiful tulip motif has been used to make a square silk scarf using pink, yellow and green paints, with outlining in gold gutta. The trace-off pattern is given here so that you can reproduce the design yourself. The tulips are set at different angles on the Habotai silk square, with a plain border and smaller tulips set at the corners. The design is very adaptable to all kinds of clothes and accessories, and could also be used to create a cushion.

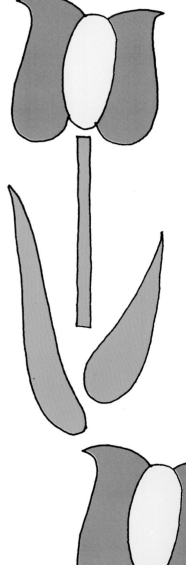

Designer tips 4

When things go wrong

Problems may arise with the smooth application of the gutta on to fabric. These can occur for several reasons:

● There may be too much air in the fluid or in the pen and this will lead to air bubbles forming as the gutta is drawn onto the fabric. Clean out the pen and replace it on the bottle, squeezing the bottle to expel any bubbles in the gutta.

● Drawing is impossible if the pen is clogged with bits of dried gutta. Disconnect the pen from the bottle and give it a thorough cleaning.

● Extremes of temperature can affect the consistency of the gutta. If it becomes too thick, it cannot flow properly through the pen. A few hours at room temperature should return the gutta to the right consistency.

Flight

This design could be interpreted as a stormy sea, powerful, turbulent and dark. The feeling of movement and the three dimensional effect are created with swirling brush strokes of paint combined with the salt technique. The sky is also turbulent, giving the impression of restless movement, and the birds and man come together in an almost surrealistic way. This is the strength of free-hand design. You can plan the general feel of a project, and design the colour scheme, but the outcome depends on your ability to give rein to your imagination. The colour scheme for Flight is striking: black and red together can be forbidding and violent, but the addition of gold gutta tempers the design and gives it a warm, rich feel. Red Habotai silk was chosen for the background. Ready-dyed fabric could be used or it could be hand-painted in advance.

Do not be afraid to experiment with different colour combinations. Try combining techniques and using different kinds of applicators to create beautiful and original pieces of work.

Below: The Butterfly was first drawn in gold gutta. Azure blue was then painted over and salt was sprinkled on the wet paint

Quilting

Quilting can considerably enhance a fabric painting providing textural contract and definition. Shadow quilting techniques described here produced the attractive cushion on the opposite page – and the gutta method is probably the most effective to combine with quilting

Quilting in the shadows

The cushion pictured shows the effect achieved when a piece of gutta painted fabric is covered with a very sheer silk. The design was transferred on to the cloth by the direct tracing method and the outline was drawn in transparent gutta. Deka silk red, black and purple paints were used. Shadowing the painted fabric with the sheer silk dramatically changes the colours. They become duskier and much softer. The technique creates an optical illusion, for, viewed from a distance, the colours merge so completely with the shadow silk that it looks as if the top silk itself is painted.

All the layers of fabric including the lining and wadding are stitched together with traditional quilting stitch. Remember to baste your fabric onto the grid base before quilting to prevent pulling and puckering. Quilting can be done in the hand or on a quilting frame.

Materials and equipment

Wadding
The type of wadding chosen depends on the effect you want to create. If a puffy effect is required to soften your work, use the polyester wadding which is available by the length.

Polyester wadding comes in several thicknesses. Use a thin wadding for small items and for clothing. The thicker waddings are better for large projects such as bed quilts and cushions.

Needles and threads
A long, thin quilting needle is used to make the traditional quilting stitch. Make sure the fabrics are basted together properly to prevent puckering and to keep the layers of cloth and wadding in place. Use thread colours which complement the colour scheme of the outer layer (Fig 1).

Stitches
Begin with a doubleback stitch on the wrong side, then bring the needle through the fabric, making sure it goes straight through and not at an angle. Pull the thread through and passing the needle down through the fabrics, make a small straight stitch, taking care to keep needle upright. Repeat this stitch to make an evenly spaced line (Fig 2).

Machine stitching
Sewing machine-stitching takes the effort out of quilting. Use a fairly large straight stitch or an open zigzag stitch.

Finishing
Remove basting threads when quilting is completed.

Free birds

This picture of birds in soft clouds was shadow quilted from behind. Sheer white silk was worked in the gutta technique with pink background paint patterned by the salt method. This softened the effect and the fluffy feel has been emphasised by the use of padding.

The shadow effect was created by backing the painted fabric with a layer of blue silk, making a subtle shadow beneath the pink. Both layers of silk were then backed with cotton and all three tacked and stitched together.

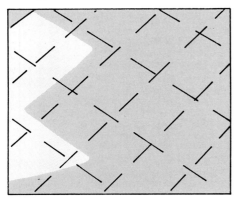

Fig 1 *Baste the layers of fabric together with vertical and horizontal stitches*

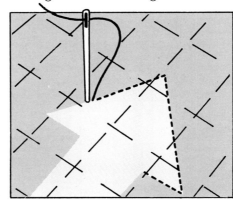

Fig 2 *When passing the needle through the fabric make sure the needle is kept upright*

The design was traced in a small,
paced quilting stitch using contrasting
mbroidery thread.

rapunta quilting

his form of quilting is done after the
esign has been stitched. For the Free
irds picture, the kapok or fibre was
tuffed between the silk and cotton
yers. The clouds were designed to
uff up, leaving the un-padded birds to
ecede into the quilting. The effect
ould be varied by stuffing the birds
stead of the clouds, but for this a
mall access slit would have to be cut in
e cotton lining as the birds are already
itched. Once quilting is completed,
e slit is sewn up.

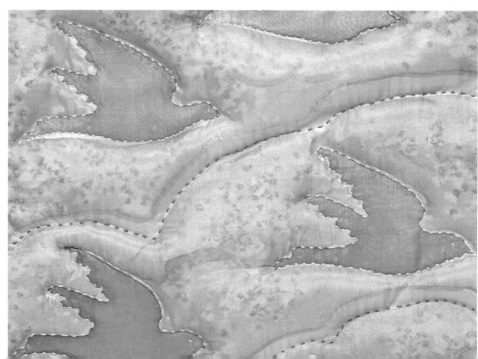

Painting on Leather

Leather is not strictly a fabric but it takes paint well and its reputation
for suppleness and strength makes it an ideal material for making
decorated leather clothing and all kinds of fashion accessories

When buying leather for painting, choose light or medium coloured hides as these show up the paint best. Most fabric paints are translucent, so unless you are working with proper leather dyes, colours will not show up on dark skins.

Materials and equipment

Leathers
First, you must find a tannery or leather merchant prepared to sell single skins. Most tanneries will only sell in bulk. Choose skins with an even quality. If a skin is thick in some places and thin in others, there will be a lot of wastage. Make sure the grain of the leather is the same all over and if it has been dyed by the tannery, check that the colouring is even. There are several types to choose from.

Kid leather
This leather is often used for glove making. It is of the finest quality, very supple and light-weight, and is suitable for both bags and clothing. Kid needs looking after, however. Treat it with special leather foods to keep it soft and long-lasting.

Calf's leather
This is also renowned for suppleness and softness, but it is stronger and tougher than kid. It is particularly popular for bags and shoes, and will last well if looked after.

Cow hide
Various types of animal are used to produce this heavy duty leather, but cows are the main source. The skins are often very poor quality, spoilt by uneven patches, but this hide is one of the cheapest available and it does respond well to careful treatment. Leather reacts like living skin: it absorbs anything put on it, so if your feed it well, it will last for many years.

Paint
Fabric paints do not need fixing when used on leather, but by mixing in a little salt, the colours will be enhanced and less likely to fade. Deka silk is well suited to leather work.

Leather tools
Of the wide variety of leather tools available, the most important are the cutting knives. Buy good quality knives and keep then sharp. A Stanley knife is an adequate substitute.

Basic technique

Transferring designs
For accuracy, draw the outline first in soft pencil which can then be painted over. If it is necessary to erase a mark, be careful with the eraser – it may remove the leather dye.

Free-hand brush drawings can be built up to form a design or stencilling is ideal for clothing, bags and belts. Sponging also works well, provided the

paint is of the right consistency. White paint can be used on dark hides if the paint is thick enough.

Patterns
Thin cardboard is better than paper for making template patterns. It is easier to work with and lasts longer.

Sewing leather

Machine sewing
Some domestic sewing machines are capable of handling leather but make sure your own machine can handle leather before you start. A heavy-duty needle should be used

Hand sewing
Leather can easily be sewn by hand, provided you have the right needles and thread. Bayonet needles are used for sewing leather, with strong, waxed thread

Leatherbags: top bag has been painted with a diagonal design in red and green. The lower bag has been lined with hand-painted striped silk.

Ideas for painted leather
Besides painting children's leather shoes in brightly coloured designs, strips of painted leather can be threaded through cut slits, or shoe laces can be made from painted strips. Scraps of coloured leather can be glued to a pair of old shoes for fun.

Painting for Patchwork

Hand-painted fabric is particularly effective when used for patchwork. Instead of searching for a range of suitable fabrics in the shades and tones you want for a project, you paint your own — and patchwork takes on a whole new dimension. In this chapter, a case for a pair of spectacles is created in colourful patchwork with additional gold embroidery.

Spectacles Case

Measure the spectacles before starting to make sure that the pattern given (Fig 1) will accommodate them comfortably. Enlarge the outlines of the pattern if necessary.

Materials and equipment
Squared graph paper
Fabrics: crêpe de chine for the patchwork, Anlung silk for the background fabric
Cotton fabric for the inner lining
Wadding, for interlining
Gold thread and gold filler thread; matching sewing thread
Paint: Deka silk paint, yellow, red and blue and gold gutta for decoration
Patchwork templates; clear plastic for fabric, metal for papers, 37mm (1 1/2in) square; 37mm (1 1/2in)-sided diamond
Tambour frame

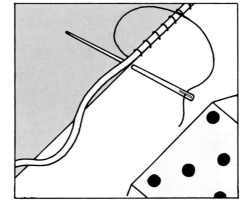

Fig 2 *Couch the gold filler thread to the case edges with neat oversewing stitches*

Preparation
Draw the pattern from Fig 1 on graph paper (scale 1 square = 2.5cm (1in). Use the outline to cut 2 shapes from the cotton fabric. Cut 2 lining pieces, cut 2 shapes in wadding. Stretch the crêpe de chine on the frame.

Trace the larger templates (used for cutting fabric) on paper, using a black felt-tipped pen. Place the tracings under the mounted crêpe de chine and trace as many shapes as required for patchwork, using the gutta pen. You will need 8 diamonds and 3 squares. When the gutta is dry, paint in the colours using the silk paints (refer to the picture for colours).
Use the smaller templates to cut a sufficient number of papers for mounting the fabric patches.
Cut out the fabric shapes (the gutta helps to prevent the fabric from fraying). Mount the fabrics on the backing paper.

Assembling the patchwork
Following the colour picture of the spectacles case, arrange the patches in the pattern and then sew them together, right sides facing, using small oversewing stitches. When all the patches are joined, press the patchwork and remove the backing papers.

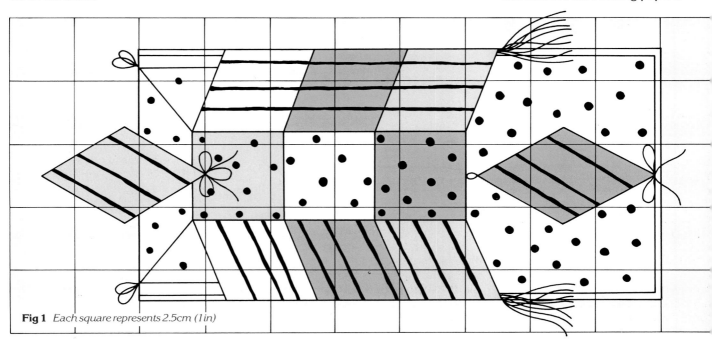

Fig 1 *Each square represents 2.5cm (1in)*

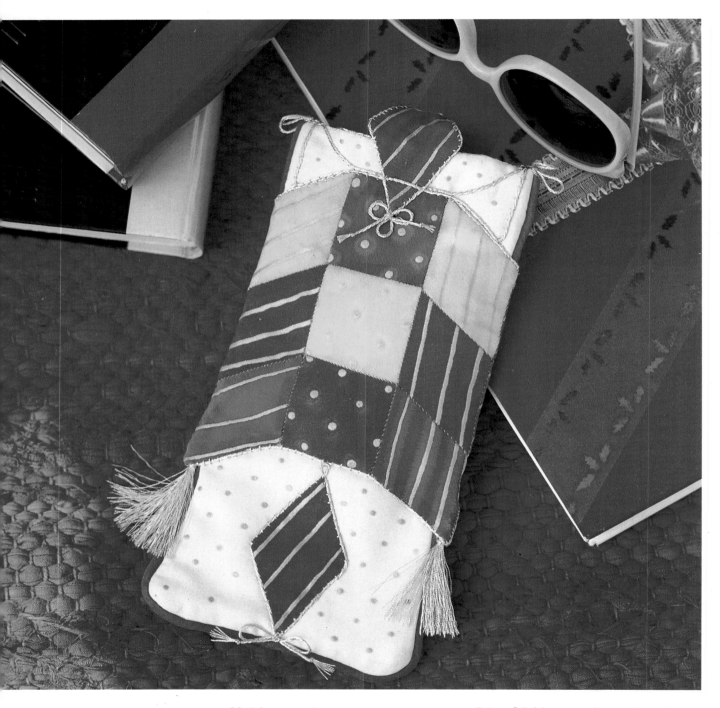

...ishing

...te the patchwork to the backing
...ic. Hand-sew the edges to the
...king. Complete the gold embroidery
...ore making up the case. Couch the
...d filler thread on the edges of the
...chwork, using a matching thread
...er to Fig 2 for the technique). Small
...d thread bows and tassels have been
...ed to enrich the design and the
...kground fabric has been further
...orated with spots of gold gutta.

Making up the case

Place the case front and back pieces
together right sides facing and
machine-stitch on the two long sides
and end, leaving the top edges open.
Turn to right side and press lightly.

Make up the lining in the same way.
Make up the wadding interfacing. Trim
the interfacing seams, slip into the case.
Slip the lining in. Round off the corners
of all fabrics. Fold in edges of outer and
lining, slipstitch.

*Below: Silk fabric was colour washed with toning
colours, then used for hexagon patchwork*

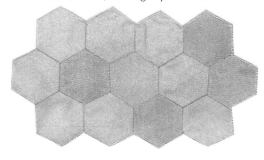

Happy feet

Rope-soled canvas shoes are a summertime favourite. Inexpensive and hard wearing, they are fun to paint, using fabric felt-tipped pens, fabric paints and gold gutta.

A collection could be built up to match a summer wardrobe. Any shoe with a cotton or canvas upper is suitable for painting, and children's plimsoles are ideal.

Materials required
Felt-tipped pens, paints
Gold gutta

Preparation
If you're decorating shoes that have been worn, make sure the fabric is clean. Scrub the fabric with warm water and household soap and leave to dry before painting. (If stains persist, a little bleach may be added to the soapy water.)

Stuff the inside of the shoes with

Left to right: Gold gutta has been used to crea design of buttons and squiggles against a dar ground; random triangle shapes in fabric pai horizontal and vertical lines in felt-tip pens; squares and random lines; a simple line patte Make sure the patterns on both shoes match.

paper to stretch the fabric smooth. Remember there is a right and a left shoe, so painted designs should resu in a matching pair.